handmade candles

Country Living

handmade candles

text by Jane Blake & Emily Paulsen

photography by Keith Scott Morton

styling by Christine Churchill

foreword by Rachel Newman

Library of Congress Cataloging-in-Publication Data
Blake, Jane.
Handmade candles : recipes for crafting candles at home / text by
    Jane Blake : photography by Keith Scott Morton : foreword by
Rachel Newman. — 1st U.S. ed.
            p. cm.
        At head of title: Contry living.
        Includes index.
        ISBN 0-688-15563-4
        1. Candlemaking. I. Country living (New York, N.Y.)
II. Title.
    TT896.5.B58   1998
    745.593' 32—dc21   97-41039
                                                    CIP

Printed in Singapore
First U.S. Edition
1 2 3 4 5 6 7 8 9 10

Text set in Galliard

Art Director: Patti Ratchford
Designer: Gretchen Mergenthaler
Editor: Camilla Crichton

Produced by Smallwood and Stewart, Inc., New York City

table of contents

foreword

At *Country Living*, we realized years ago that the best way to add mood, romance, and warmth to a room was with candlelight. And this stands to reason, considering the seventeenth- and eighteenth-century roots of the country style. Candles are so evocative of those earlier, less complicated times—of nights when they were the only source of light. Of course, now we depend on electric lighting; but candles still have a place in our homes—one of the most important challenges in making a decorating scheme work is the proper use and placement of lighting, and this means candles as well as overhead lights and table lamps.

Candles can bring life to any corner. The creative home owners whose candles are pictured here are not content with having candles in just the obvious places; they have found a use for them in every room of the house, as well as on the porch and in the garden.

The pleasure we take from a candle is all the greater for its simplicity. What we hope to share with you in this new book is the pleasure of making candles yourself, for your home and to give to family and friends. We think you will find the candles on the pages that follow easy and fun to create. Their colors can be glorious, their shapes far more interesting than those you can buy at the store. And you may discover that making candles becomes a new ritual for you, one that friends can join in, perhaps to make candles for a wedding-table centerpiece, a Fourth of July block party, or gifts to give at Christmas.

Now we invite you to enjoy with us this enduring symbol of country warmth.

—Rachel Newman, Editor-in-Chief

introduction

Near my home in upstate New York, there's a wonderful community tradition that was started by one family about ten years ago. One Christmas Eve, they lined their section of the road with luminaria they had fashioned out of plastic milk jugs. The next year, several of their neighbors did the same thing along their properties. Each succeeding year, more and more people decided to join in the effort. Now there are more than twenty-five miles of road lit by candlelight on that special night. It's a breathtaking experience to drive slowly along the country lanes following the path created by hundreds of luminaria.

This is but one example of how candlelight transforms the ordinary into the extraordinary. Beginning with a solitary candle atop one's first birthday cake, candles figure prominently in our lives. We use them to mark special occasions, decorate our homes, and to add a touch of romance to everyday life. Of course, although candles remain important in our modern lives, it's hard to imagine the vital role candlelight played in the daily lives of our ancestors. The only glimpse we get is when our electricity goes out in a storm. Although flashlights are an easier way to break the darkness, most of us still have a stash of candle stubs ready to light, just in case of a power outage. One candle can make a world of difference on a dark and stormy night.

Imagine what it was like when candles were one of the few sources of light. Then, the day-to-day schedules that most people kept followed the movement of the sun. During the long, cold nights of winter, lighting a candle did more than light the night. It made people more productive and allowed entertainment to continue way past sundown—candlelight challenged the forces of nature, if only for a little while. It's no accident, therefore, that our most beloved and traditional holidays—such as Christmas, Chanukah, and Halloween—revolve around candlelight.

Since Roman days, beeswax has been the most sought-after candle-making ingredient. This soft, sticky honey by-product burns clean and long and has a lovely aroma. But beeswax has always come with a hefty price tag, so most people were forced to seek out alternatives, or simply did without.

From the Middle Ages onward, candles for the masses were made from tallow (rendered animal fat) which was melted and poured into metal molds. When available, some whale fat or vegetable fat was added to improve the quality of the candle. Tallow may have put candlelight within reach, but there was a catch—although an improvement on sitting in darkness, these candles gave off an unpleasant odor and left a greasy residue.

Candles made of vegetable waxes, such as bayberry (popular in colonial America) and carnauba wax (used in Brazil), were much preferred to tallow candles. They had the advantage of natural color and scent, but were unfortunately difficult to produce on a large scale. So candles made from these waxes were saved for special occasions.

Then in the 1800s, it was discovered that adding stearin (a naturally occurring fatty acid) to tallow enhanced candle hardness, lengthened burn time, and reduced the problem of odor and residue. Not long afterwards, paraffin wax was developed as a by-product of the evolving petroleum industry. By combining man-made ingredients with natural waxes, such as beeswax and bayberry, candles at last became a pleasant and affordable source of light for everyone.

The prevalence of candles, however, hasn't diminished the sense of luxury and romance we feel whenever we light them. In this age of neon lights and cities that never sleep, candlelight still signifies mystery and miracles. Perhaps it is because of the technological age that we live in that candlelight has become more precious—harkening back to simpler, less fast-paced times.

Handmade candles are even more special. Just like a hand-sewn quilt or home-baked bread, handmade candles exude the personality of their maker and the quality of their ingredients. Making candles is also a great escape from today's high-tech world. Candle-making can be a solitary process—a quiet time with your thoughts and your creativity—or, you can get together with friends and inspire each other to even greater heights of ingenuity.

Best of all, handmade candles aren't difficult to make—some of the recipes in this book are superbly easy. Others take a bit more skill and patience; but not much. In Chapter One, the basic candle-making techniques are described, along with the ingredients and equipment you'll need. Then, in the succeeding chapters, there are recipes for making candles for inside your home, outside your home, and for special occasions.

chapter one

the basic recipes

Wax and wick: that's the essence of candles. But what variations you can spin off that basic theme! When you think of all the different candles you've seen and admired—all the shapes and sizes, colors and combinations—it's hard to believe that most of them were created using one of three basic methods: rolling, dipping, or molding. Rolled candles involve a sheet of wax that you roll up around a wick. To make a dipped candle, you repeatedly dip the wick into hot wax, slowly building up a candle layer by layer. For molded candles, you simply pour molten wax into a mold and leave it to harden.

It takes just a few basic ingredients and tools to make candles by hand. Waxes and other materials are available at most craft, art supply, and even some hardware and variety stores. You probably have most of the equipment in your kitchen already. The rest can easily be purchased through craft stores and mail order companies. (A list of suppliers appears on page 108.)

Once you've assembled what you need and mastered the Basic Recipes, you can make a wide variety of candles that will complement your decor, enhance outdoor living space, and celebrate special occasions.

ingredients

Although it is beeswax that makes the best and most beautiful candles, it can be costly and hard to come by. However, today we have the advantage of being able to combine natural waxes with the cheaper, more readily available man-made varieties—even if a recipe calls for just paraffin wax, or just beeswax, it's worth adding a bit of the other. The result will be enchanting and versatile candles, that make the most of their ingredients.

wick—the wick is the conduit that supplies the flame with a constant stream of wax. The best wicks are made of tightly woven cotton fibers. The spaces between the fibers act as tiny capillaries, supplying the flame with a constant, but not over-abundant, supply of wax. The diameter of the candle determines the thickness of the wick. If a wick is too thin for the width of the candle, it will not supply enough wax to the flame, and your candle will flicker and eventually go out. If, on the other hand, the wick is too thick, it will flood the flame with melted wax—an equally undesirable result.

Wicks come in three types: flat braid (for dipped candles), square braid (for molded and rolled candles), and wire-core (for long-burning candles, such as container candles and sand

candles). When you buy wick, you will find that the package the wick comes in will suggest a suitable candle-diameter. Follow the manufacturer's instructions, but when in doubt, follow these guidelines: for small candles (three-quarters of an inch or less in diameter), use size 4/0. For candles up to two inches in diameter, use size 2/0. For candles with a diameter of two to three inches, use a #1 wick. Use a #2 wick for a candle-diameter of three to four

Most people think a candle flame is produced by the burning wick, but actually the wick is the fuel delivery system. The wax is the fuel, and it is the wax that burns to produce the flame. In fact, only the addition of chemicals to wicks allows them to burn along with the wax. Early candles used plain cotton fiber wicks, and the wicks actually had to be trimmed as the wax burned down.

When you strike a match, the carbon molecules in the tip become charged and produce light rays. However, without a constant source of fuel, the match burns out quickly. A candle extends the life of the flame by constantly feeding it fuel—hot wax. It is the combustion of that wax which produces light. The wax and wick work together: the tiny fibers of the wick form capillaries that supply melted wax to keep the flame steady and bright.

inches, and #3 wicks are recommended for candles with a diameter of more than four inches.

Wick comes in rolls or in pre-cut lengths. Although they are still made of cotton threads, most commercially available wicks are treated with substances that allow the wick to burn along with the wax.

The last step in candle-making is trimming the wick. It should be cut so it extends no more than about a quarter of an inch above the top of the candle.

wax—the three most common types of wax used in candle-making are beeswax, paraffin wax, and dip-and-carve wax.

Totally natural and with a sweet aroma, beeswax adds softness and beauty to candles and also increases burning time. Honeybees secrete this soft, sticky wax to seal up the cells of their honeycomb to preserve the honey for the winter. Of course, such a desirable substance does not come cheap—so shop around and make use of the suppliers on page 108.

Beeswax comes in one-pound blocks or sheets, which are perfect for easy and impressive-looking rolled candles. The rectangular sheets measure about 8 x 16 inches and are available in natural taupe, bleached white, and in a variety of dyed hues. One sheet makes a candle eight inches tall and just over an inch and a half in diameter, or two candles just

For all candles except dipped and rolled candles, you must first "prime" the wick with a bit of wax. This helps get the wick burning before the candle has a chance to start melting. You can buy pre-primed wicks, or you can do it yourself by dipping a length of wick in melted paraffin wax for about 20 seconds. Lay it straight on a waxed paper–lined cookie sheet to dry.

In dipped candles, the first dip actually acts to prime the wick. You simply dip a little deeper the first time round. In rolled candles, a small piece of beeswax pressed around the wick tip is enough to prime the wick. Alternatively, you can dip the end in a bit of melted paraffin.

under an inch in diameter. You can roll wider candles by pressing wax sheets together.

Beeswax can be used alone or in combination with other waxes, so if you have leftover bits from beeswax sheets after making rolled candles, you can save them to add to the melting pot for your next molded or dipped candle-making project. Adding beeswax to other commonly used waxes (paraffin and dip-and-carve, see page 18) will both soften colors and enhance burning time.

Beeswax is naturally sticky, so there are a few rules of thumb that will facilitate working with it. When using beeswax for molded candles, first treat the mold with a releasing agent (such as silicone spray, see page 24) to make it easier to remove the candle. Also, if you keep the temperature of the beeswax below 160°F when pouring a candle, the wax will not stick as much.

Because beeswax is naturally opaque, there's no need for opaque crystals (see opposite page) in one hundred percent beeswax candles. Even stearin (see opposite page) is not necessary as long as you follow the temperature guidelines above (i.e. 160°F) and take the precaution of spritzing the mold with silicone spray before pouring the wax.

The primary ingredient in most recipes for molded candles is paraffin wax. Not only is it much less expensive and more widely available than other types of wax, it is also colorless and odorless, making it an ideal substrate (carrier) for dyes and fragrances. It's also harder than beeswax and produces a candle with a sheen. When combining beeswax with paraffin wax, use a ratio of one to ten. This small amount of beeswax shouldn't cause any sticking problems for molded candles.

Paraffin, a by-product of the oil refinement process, comes in ten or twelve-pound blocks or in granular form. It is also available with ten percent stearin already added. The granular type melts faster, but the blocks can be broken into pieces to create some of the easiest and most dramatic-looking homemade candles (see page 72).

Candle-making supply stores and mail order companies often carry different types of paraffin, classified by the temperature at which the wax melts and the pliability of the wax at room temperature. The best paraffin for most candle-making projects melts at 135°F to 140°F, but you'll still need to heat the wax to 160°F or more for most recipes. The exact temperature is determined by the candle-making method you're using, the mold material (see the section on Pouring Temperatures on page 23), and the final effect you want to achieve.

A blend of paraffin with other waxes, dip-and-carve wax is made to be a bit softer than ordinary paraffin wax, so it won't crack when it is carved. It's especially well suited for dipped candles; the softer quality helps the layers of wax to adhere to each other. It's also the best wax for carving special effects into candles.

Other natural waxes—before the development of paraffin, people depended on natural waxes and fats to make candles. Wax occurs naturally in almost all living things, and theoretically any type of wax could be used to make candles. Unfortunately, the overharvesting of wax from animals and plants has threatened many species. Many natural waxes are therefore no longer available or very scarce.

Tallow, made from animal fat, may be a natural and traditional ingredient, but that doesn't mean you'll want to use the drippings from your next roast to make candles. Commercial candle-makers continue to use some refined tallow (usually from beef fat) in selected candles. Though longer burning than paraffin, and not as odoriferous as the tallow used in Medieval times, refined tallow is not readily available to amateur candlemakers.

Another natural wax that was quite popular came from sperm whales. However, to obtain a significant amount of this wax, the whale has to be killed. Since they are a protected species in the United States, this wax is no longer available.

One of the most coveted types of natural wax is bayberry. The early Americans discovered that the berries of the bayberry shrub (*myrica pennsylvanica* or *myrica cerifera*) are coated with a lovely greenish blue wax, which produces excellent aromatic candles. Despite the fact that the wax is difficult to separate from the rest of the plant—the berries must be boiled in water so that the wax coating floats to the surface—the demand for bayberry candles was strong. In particular, bayberry candles were used at Christmas-time in colonial America—burning one on Christmas Eve was supposed to bring good luck. In their quest to produce bayberry candles cost-effectively, harvesters carelessly cut off branches and leaves along with the berries—thereby killing the bushes. The result is that today the bayberry bush is a rare and protected species in the United States, and the small amount of bayberry wax available to candle-makers is imported from other countries.

other ingredients—

these are the ingredients that you will need in addition to wax and wick for creating beautiful candles.

Also called stearic acid, stearin is a concentrated fatty acid derived from animal fat. It is available as a white, flaky powder, resembling laundry detergent. The addition of stearin to paraffin wax helps it harden and shrink, making the candle easier to release from the mold. It also adds opacity, reduces drips when burning, and gives the candle a nice sheen. But take care not to use too much or your candle will begin to look soapy or chalky. A ratio of ten to one, paraffin wax to stearin, usually gives the best results. To use stearin, melt it first—it goes from solid to liquid very quickly. If you're using a dye, mix it with the stearin before adding the wax. This hastens the melting process and helps distribute the dye more evenly throughout the wax.

Add opaque crystals to paraffin wax to make your white candles whiter and your dyed candles clearer. They are especially important to prevent air-cooled and scented candles from spotting. Use a half to one full teaspoon per one pound paraffin wax. Opaque crystals melt at a higher temperature than stearin or paraffin, so melt the crystals with a small amount of the wax first, and then add the remainder of the wax. (If you wait until later to add the crystals, you'll have to heat the entire batch of wax to that higher temperature.) Since opaque crystals also harden wax, there is no reason to use them in concert with stearin.

Also called wick sustainers or wick supports, wick holders anchor wicks to the bottom of container candles. They consist of a small square of metal with a hole in the middle. Simply insert the wick into the hole and pinch the holder together to hold the wick in place.

Small squares or disks of concentrated colored wax, wax dyes can be melted with stearin or by themselves in order to color paraffin wax. Dyes can be mixed to produce interesting, custom colors—in much the same way you mix paint colors to get the shade you want. A guiding rule is that one dye square or disk will color one pound wax. The amount you actually use will depend on the depth of color you are aiming for. Also, if you are doing an over-dip (dipping an already-made candle in a different color wax), you must use at least four times the usual amount of dye. Most colors will become lighter as the wax hardens, and some colors and brands will change more than others. A bit of trial and error is part and parcel of creating colored candles.

Added to melted wax before pouring or dipping, candle scent can be purchased in small squares, similar to wax dye, or in liquid form. You can also use essential oils, available in aromatherapy and natural food stores. Choose carefully, however, because not all essential oils burn well. Use these scents sparingly; a few drops is all you need for one pound of wax. A little will add a bit of spice to your creation— this is one case where less is more. (For more on scenting candles, see page 44.)

Similar to a glue stick, use a dab of stick-um™ to attach decorations to candles or to glue pieces of wax together. (It's also great for making candles stand up straight in ill-fitting candleholders!) As an alternative, you can also use melted paraffin wax in the same way. Just melt a small amount in the top of a double boiler and apply to the candle with a small, soft paintbrush.

equipment

You can buy candle-making equipment, or you can resurrect some old kitchen equipment. That beat-up baking pan or percolator in the back of the cupboard may be just what you need to create excellent candles. Pick up old pots and pans at yard sales and second-hand shops and dedicate them to your candle-making.

You will need a rimmed cookie sheet (or baking pan) for laying out primed wicks, salvaging unused wax, and creating homemade wax sheets. An old cookie sheet or jelly-roll pan (9 x 18 inches) is one of the most useful pieces of candle-making equipment. Choose one (or more) with high sides—about three-quarters of an inch—so it will hold wax.

Although you can jerry-rig a double boiler by using two pots, or a bowl and a saucepan, a true double boiler heats the wax more evenly and helps prevent it from reaching temperatures above 212°F (water's boiling point). Choose a stainless steel, aluminum, or enamel-coated set; something heavy and solid will work best. When using, check occasionally to make sure there is adequate water remaining in the bottom of the pan. After you pour the melted wax into a mold or onto a cookie sheet for future use, clean the top of the double boiler by wiping it with a dry dish towel before the wax residue hardens.

You can buy a special dipping can at a crafts shop, or you can improvise with an old percolator, metal pitcher, or other tall, narrow, cylindrical pot. A dipping can is used to hold the melted wax when dipping or overdipping candles. The container needs to be at least two inches taller than the candle you are creating. In order to melt the wax and keep it hot while you dip, set the can in the bottom of a double boiler or other pan of boiling water. Choose a pan with high sides, since the water will ensure the wax stays at a relatively consistent temperature.

Reaching and maintaining the right temperature is the key to creating beautiful candles. Therefore, you need to have an accurate thermometer. A candy or cooking thermometer will do as long as it registers temperatures between 100°F and 225°F. A temperature of 160°F to 180°F is ideal for making most types of candles. Occasionally, though, you'll need to heat the wax to higher temperatures—be extra careful in these cases: hot wax can catch fire just like grease or cooking oil (usually at about 375°F). See the section on candle-making safety, page 25.

For weighing out wax and other materials, a good scale comes in very handy. For

amounts of less than five pounds or so, a postal scale will do the job. These are generally inexpensive and available at office supply stores. You can also look for scales at hardware and craft stores.

Specially designed candle molds are available at most craft stores. They come in a wide variety of shapes and sizes. Glass, acrylic, and metal molds can be used again and again—at ideal temperatures, the wax will not crack them. Rubber ones don't last as long, but are available in a greater range of designs. Finding and choosing molds is also a great place to let your creativity loose. Tin cans, cake pans, Jell-O molds, seashells, and other found items can all make wonderful candle molds and holders for container candles. To work out how much wax you'll need to fill a found mold, fill the mold with water, then pour the water into a measuring cup. You need approximately three ounces wax for every three and one half ounces water. You can find out the best pouring temperature for your found mold by using the guidelines opposite.

Called wicking needles, these heavy-duty steel needles come in four to ten-inch lengths and are used at several stages in candle-making. For example, they can be used to wick an already molded candle (such as on page 66), to prick the surface of a candle before topping off (see page 30) with addi-

Pouring temperatures are geared to the type of wax and the mold used in a recipe or to the desired effect. If you want to create your own candle recipes, you need to know about pouring temperatures. When you buy a mold, follow the manufacturer's guide for the best pouring temperature. Otherwise, always err on the side of caution—if a candle doesn't come out the way you want, melt it down and try again at a higher temperature. Here are some guidelines that may help you when developing your own ideas:

Molded beeswax: to prevent sticking, pour beeswax no hotter than 160°F into the mold.

Dipped candles: maintain the wax temperature at 160°F to produce consistent layers. To give the final layer a nice sheen, raise the temperature to 180°F.

Acrylic molds: these are resilient molds, so pour at 200°F for the best results.

Cardboard or paper molds: for plain cardboard or paper, keep the temperature low—160°F. The exception is ice candles (see page 60), where ice lowers the wax temperature, so you need to heat to 200°F.

Foil: foil can withstand higher temperatures— 180°F to 200°F works well.

Metal molds: aim for a pouring temperature of about 190°F.

tional wax, or as "tie rods"—to hold the wick in place when making molded candles.

For just about any candle recipe, you'll need a stirrer to mix in dye or scents, or just to make sure the wax melts evenly in the pot. A wooden spoon or chopstick works best. Before using, ensure that there are no jagged edges or splintery parts that could break off and contaminate the wax.

You will also need cutting tools: a sharp craft knife (matte knife) or other cutting implement to cut beeswax sheets, to trim wicks, and to cut templates or stencils, etc. For carved candles, a set of cutting tools like those used for woodcuts or engravings is recommended.

A pitcher or pouring pot is also needed for pouring the melted wax into a mold. If you're working with small containers or molds, then a smaller pitcher is best—such as the bottom of a stove-top espresso maker. You can buy specially designed pouring pots at craft stores, or you can select an old pitcher from your cupboard. Make sure it does not have any seams that could leak. Once used for candle-making, the pot will need to be carefully cleaned before being used for food preparation.

A heat source is needed for melting the wax. You can heat wax on your kitchen stove, but a hot plate will work just as well. If you don't have a hot plate, a camp stove will do—just make sure you have adequate control over the temperature or flame size. For rolled candles, an ordinary hand-held hairdryer is all you need to slightly soften the wax sheets.

Whatever your heat source, use caution to avoid burns when working with heated materials and equipment. Keep potholders and trivets nearby for handling hot pots and pans. And never leave melted wax unattended.

Similar to putty, mold seal is used to seal molds and containers to prevent leakage of wax through wick holes and other gaps. It can be used again and again.

Use waxed paper to line cookie sheets, or to shield candles from your fingers when you are dealing with soft wax. It's also a good idea to cover your work area with waxed paper. It will protect your furniture from the hot wax, and any spilled wax can be removed easily from the paper and remelted for your next creation.

Finally, use silicone spray as a releasing agent to make molds easier to remove. This greaseless spray is similar to Teflon and is available at hardware stores.

safety in the candle kitchen

As with cooking or any other activity involving heated materials and equipment, there is some risk of burns and fires in candle-making. However, with proper precautions and careful preparation, you can safely enjoy creating masterpieces in wax.

Unless the recipe specifies otherwise, always use a double boiler to melt wax and replenish the water as necessary. Wax heated over boiling water will not rise above 212°F (water's boiling point) and most of the recipes in this book will not require you to heat wax higher than this temperature.

Always use a wax thermometer with a gauge that reads up to 225°F, and try to avoid allowing the wax to heat to temperatures above 200°F. (If your thermometer is pegged at 225°F, don't try to guess how hot the wax really is. Turn off the heat and remove the wax from the heat source.) Most of the recipes in this book do not require such high temperatures, but when they do, be especially vigilant. Wax does not boil, but it will catch fire at higher temperatures—usually above 375°F. (The exact temperature depends on the ingredients of the wax blend.)

If a wax fire does occur, turn off the heat immediately and cover the pan with a damp cloth, or slide a lid onto the pot. (Never place the lid straight down on a flaming pot. Air currents will force the flames out and around to your hand.) Do not attempt to put out a wax fire with water or flour. Sand or baking soda may help, as will a dry chemical fire extinguisher.

Never leave melting wax unattended, and keep small children and pets away from the work area. Always be sure to use potholders, gloves, and trivets when handling hot containers and hot wax.

Never pour melted wax down the drain. As it cools, it will harden and clog the pipes. Any leftover wax can be poured onto a cookie sheet lined with waxed paper and allowed to cool. It can then be remelted and used again.

If hot wax spills onto your skin, submerge the affected area in water, peel off the wax, and treat as you would any other burn: try to keep the burned area elevated above heart-level, and make sure you remove clothing and jewelry near the burn in case of swelling. Hold the affected area under cold running water or apply cold compresses (a pack of frozen peas works well). If the burn covers more than two inches of skin, call a doctor or go to the emergency room.

basic recipe
rolled candles

Although rolled candles are by far the easiest candles to make—you simply roll up a sheet of wax around a wick—they create a lasting impression. Paraffin wax is available in sheets, but beeswax is much easier to work with. The cross-hatched surface of beeswax sheets also adds distinctive flair.

1. With a straightedge as a guide and a craft knife, cut the beeswax sheet into two 8-inch squares.

2. Use a hairdryer to slightly soften the wax. Avoid over-softening the wax by using the low heat or "style" setting.

3. Press the wick into one of the edges of a wax square; 1 inch of wick should extend beyond each side. Roll up the wax, taking care to keep the edges even. It can be a little tricky to get started and to keep the roll tight around the wick; to get a tighter roll, insert a piece of waxed paper between your fingers and the wax. As you roll the wax, move the waxed paper along so it doesn't get caught up in the roll. This not only gives a tighter roll, but it also prevents the heat of your hands from making the wax too soft and therefore difficult to work with.

4. When the candle is completely rolled, press the edge of the wax into the candle to seal it, softening it with the hairdryer if necessary.

5. Repeat steps 3 and 4 with the second square.

6. To prime the wicks, take small pieces of wax sheet and press them around the wicks. Alternatively, in the top of a double boiler over medium heat, melt the paraffin wax. Dip the wick ends into the wax for 5 seconds and allow to cool completely.

7. Trim the wicks to 1/4 inch and the candles are ready to light.

One 8 x 16-inch beeswax sheet

One 10-inch length braided 2/0 wick

1 to 2 ounces paraffin wax for priming the wick, if desired

basic recipe
molded candles

You can make molded candles in all sorts of shapes and sizes. For some, you will want to remove the mold to reveal the candle. In others, the container itself becomes an integral part of the final creation. This recipe makes a good-size candle—it's not so small that it's difficult to handle, and it's not so big as to be overpowering. It's perfect for decorating, or for over-dipping and carving. I've specified beeswax, but you can just as easily use paraffin. In fact, if want to scent or color the candle, paraffin is preferable. Just be sure to add ten percent stearin (in this case 0.8 ounce), and to heat the wax to around 190°F.

1. Prepare the mold—you will need one 7 x 2-inch mold. Ensure it is clean and dry. The mold should be at room temperature or slightly warmer when you pour in the wax. A squirt of silicon spray will ensure the candle will unmold easily.

2. Wick the mold by threading the wick through the hole at the bottom and pulling it through to the top of the mold. Tie the top to a wicking needle and rest it on the top of the mold—forming a "tie rod." Turn the mold over, center the wick, pull it taut, and secure it with plenty of mold seal. You can also put a piece of masking tape over the mold seal just to make certain! Seal up any cracks in the mold with mold seal. (Metal molds are best sealed with specially designed magnetic seal. If that's not available, use regular mold seal, but remember that since metal conducts heat faster than plastic, the seal may loosen.)

3. In the top of a double boiler over medium heat, melt the beeswax.

4. Heat the beeswax to 160°F. (If you are using paraffin wax, make sure

9-inch length #1 wick, primed

0.5 pound beeswax

you add stearin first and heat the mixture to 190°F.) Remember that different mold materials call for different wax temperatures. If a different temperature is specified on the mold you are using, go by that temperature. Also, refer to the Pouring Temperatures guide on page 23. Remember, when using beeswax, that pouring at temperatures above 160°F may cause a candle to stick in the mold; although silicone spray will help to prevent this. Once heated to the correct temperature, transfer the wax to a pouring jug.

5. Holding the mold at an angle (this helps to prevent the formation of air bubbles), pour the wax into the mold. As it fills, gradually tip the mold back to an upright position. Fill to about 1/2 inch from top of the mold.

6. To release any trapped air bubbles, tap the sides of the mold lightly, or gently stir with a narrow stick or wicking needle, scraping the sides of the mold. The cooler temperature of the mold can cause the wax to harden unevenly—which is why it is important to warm the mold to room temperature before you begin. Stirring the wax ensures that the candle hardens more uniformly. Don't be tempted to skip this step; it's essential for getting the best results.

7. Allow the candle to cool in the mold for about an hour.

8. During cooling, the wax may shrink, causing a slight indent to form around the wick. To remedy this, take a wicking needle and make several pricks in the indent. Over medium heat, remelt and heat the remaining wax to 160°F (or the temperature you're using), and "top off" the candle—refill the indent. Leave the candle to cool for 30 minutes to an hour. If necessary, repeat the topping off process until you achieve a level surface. A funnel or small pouring pitcher is ideal for this procedure.

9. Set the candle aside for 6 to 8 hours, until it has cooled completely and has begun to pull away from the sides of the mold. To unmold it,

first remove the mold seal from the bottom of the mold, then use the tie rod to pull the candle out of the mold. You may need to tap the sides lightly to help release the candle. If you have trouble releasing the candle from the mold, place it in the refrigerator for 20 minutes. This will shrink the wax and the candle should slide out easily.

10. Remove the tie rod and cut off the wick slightly below the surface of the wax. This is the bottom of the candle.

11. To ensure a completely level bottom on which the candle will stand upright and securely, line a frying pan with foil and place the pan over high heat. When it is very hot, turn off the heat and place the candle on the hot foil. Rotate the candle for a few seconds to even off the base.

12. Finally, trim the wick to $\frac{1}{4}$ inch and the candles are ready to light.

Container candles are made in much the same way as molded candles —except the candle remains in the container. Almost anything can make a suitable container for candles: pretty tins (see page 41), jars, and votive glasses make excellent containers. Even items found in nature can be filled with wax and turned into candles. Try hollowed-out sticks, eggshells, and seashells (see pages 84 and 78). Use a wire-core wick and wick holder for these candles, and anchor it in the bottom of the container by pouring in enough wax to fill the first $\frac{1}{2}$ inch of the container. When the wax has cooled, wrap the end of the wick around a tie rod and rest the rod on the top of the container. Take up any slack in the wick and center it, being careful not to dislodge the other end of the wick. Fill the container with wax and allow to cool. Top off as necessary, and when fully cooled, remove the tie rod and trim the wick to $\frac{1}{4}$ inch.

basic recipe
dipped candles

At living history museums, candle dipping demonstrations always draw a crowd. With candles hanging from a wheel suspended from the ceiling, it is fascinating to watch the candlemaker removing each pair, one by one, and dipping them into the wax. With each dip, the candles gradually take shape. Even though the process can be long and repetitive, the rhythm of the work is soothing. For dipping candles, you need to allow an extra four inches in the wick length for holding and hanging the candle pair.

4 pounds beeswax

Three 24-inch lengths flat-braided 2/0 wick

1. In a 12-inch dipping can, set in the bottom of a double boiler over medium heat, melt the wax. Heat to 160°F.

2. Start dipping your candle pairs: drape a wick over 3 fingers so the sides hang separately and evenly. Dip the lower 10½ inches of wick into the wax and hold for 10 seconds. Remove the wick and hang it on a rod or over two nails to dry. If necessary, straighten the wicks. (This primes the wick and applies the first layer of the candle.)

3. Repeat step 2 with the other lengths of wick. Be sure to check the wax temperature several times to ensure you maintain 160°F.

4. Now, go back to your first pair. This time, you'll dip only the lower 10 inches of wick to create a 10-inch candle. Continue dipping until the candle diameter measures ¾ inch (about 30 dips), then dip once more.

5. To give the outside of the candle a smooth, clean finish, bring the wax temperature up to 180°F. Dip each pair for 3 seconds. Allow the candles to cool for 4 minutes.

6. Trim the base of the finished candles with a sharp knife. (To ensure that you don't leave imprints, put a sheet of waxed paper between

your fingers and the candles.) Return the candles to the drying rack and leave to cool for several hours or overnight.

5. Trim the wicks to ¼ inch and the candles are ready to light.

Dipping works best if you make several pairs at a time. You can fashion a drying rack by hammering pairs of nails into a board or by suspending a dowel or slat between two chairs. Or, if you have a hanging pot rack, suspend the pairs from that.

Because you must keep the wax in the dipping can to a depth of at least 10 inches, you'll melt a lot more wax when making dipped candles than you'll actually use. But that doesn't mean there has to be lots of waste. Pour the extra wax off into an old coffee can or other container and save it for your next candle-making project.

The optimum drying time between dips depends on your workroom temperature: the cooler the room, the shorter the drying time. For the best results, dip the candles while the previous layer is still just slightly tacky. If you are interrupted in the midst of your dipping project, and must leave the candles for several hours or even days, start again with an initial dip at a higher temperature—about 180°F—and hold the candle in the wax a bit longer. This will remove the last layer of wax and heat the candle so it can receive new wax.

As you add layers to your candles, you may need to add wax to your dipping can. If you find you're "hitting bottom" when you dip your candles, add more wax, melt and heat back to 160°F, and continue. As you work, be sure to check the wax temperature every so often. Candles dipped at too cool a temperature will appear lumpy, while if the wax is too hot the previous layer will be removed (which you only want to do when you are restarting after a break or when you are done and want to put a final gloss on the finished candles).

tips for making & using candles

a candle kitchen—

If you have room, it's worth creating a space devoted to candle-making. A utility area, with a sink and electric outlet for your hot plate, would be ideal. But if there's no sink, don't despair; a bucket of water or a garden hose should be all you'll ever need.

You also need a place to store your ingredients and equipment. You'll find that you end up with quite a lot of leftover wax—which is well worth keeping and re-using. Label the boxes of leftover wax, clearly indicating the proportion of paraffin to beeswax to stearin, etc., so that you know what you're dealing with next time around.

cleaning up—even the most

careful candle-maker occasionally drips or spills a little hot wax. Here are some tips to help you clean up:

- Line your work area—including floors—with newspaper, then cover with waxed paper. Any spilled wax can then be peeled off the waxed paper and re-used.
- Use white spirit or turpentine to remove small spots of wax on molds or containers. (You may want to spot test to ensure that it does not damage containers.)
- If wax splashes onto clothing or carpets,

leave it to harden. Scrape away most of the wax, then remove the remainder by covering the area with a paper towel and ironing with a warm iron. If any stain remains, use a dry-cleaning solution to remove it.

burning & storing

- To increase burning time, put candles in the refrigerator half an hour before lighting.
- Keep candle wicks trimmed to $1/4$ inch.
- Store candles in a cool, dry place, out of direct sunlight.
- Buff candles with a nylon stocking to remove dust or marks.
- Protect furniture, tablecloths, and other surfaces from dripping wax, by placing candleholders on a plate, or other fireproof surface.
- Never leave burning candles unattended.
- Ensure that curtains, flower bouquets, and other decorations (including those on the candle) are kept away from the flame.
- To prevent splattering, keep lit candles out of drafts, and use a snuffer to extinguish them (or hold your hand on the other side of the flame and blow gently).
- Never let a candle burn to within an inch of its holder.

chapter two

candles in the home

Candlelight affects us in so many ways—softening mood, adding romance and mystery, and brightening the figurative, as well as the literal, darkness.

Dinner by candlelight is a time-honored way to celebrate. But why wait for a special occasion? Candles at the family dinner table somehow make conversations more civilized. Candlelight transforms the ordinary into the magical anywhere in your home. Watching classic black-and-white movies by candlelight is deliciously romantic.

Candles are also utilitarian. Light a "kitchen candle" to absorb cooking smells, for example, and on rainy days, a burning candle will take some of the humidity out of the air. And what about turning an ordinary bath into a luxurious experience by evaporating essential oil in a burner over a votive?

You don't even have to light candles to enjoy their contribution to your living space. Hand-dipped candle pairs look wonderful draped over a peg, or display bundled tapers tied with ribbon on open shelves. Best of all, exhibiting your candles puts them within easy reach when you want to enjoy their special light

rolled tapers

Just a simple variation on Basic Recipe Rolled Candles, these charming tapers combine a homemade touch with a feeling of elegance. Use them as an accent on your dining table, or place them on the coffee table and serve dessert in the living room. (Use the leftover pieces of wax sheet from this recipe to make miniature rolled candles that look spectacular in perfume or cordial bottles.)

1. Using a straightedge as a guide and a craft knife, cut the beeswax sheet into two 8-inch squares.

   One 8 x 16-inch beeswax sheet

   Two 10-inch lengths 2/0 square-braided wick

2. Place one of the squares in front of you, and position the straightedge diagonally from the top left corner to the middle of the right-hand edge. Using the craft knife, cut along the straightedge and peel away the smaller of the two shapes.

3. Rotate the larger triangle 90° counter-clockwise and press a length of wick along the bottom edge; 1 inch of wick should extend beyond each side.

4. If necessary, use a hairdryer to slightly soften the wax. Roll up the candle, taking care to keep the edges along the bottom even (the right-hand edge). To achieve a tighter roll, insert a piece of waxed paper between your fingers and the wax. When the candle is completely rolled, press the edge of the wax into the candle to seal.

5. Repeat steps 2 through 4 with the second square of wax.

6. Prime and trim the wicks before lighting the candles.

candles in tins

Tea tins are ideal for making these simple but effective container candles. However, wonderful container candles can also be made from olive oil tins and even sardine cans. If you travel abroad, pick up inexpensive tins in grocery stores to fill with wax—the candles make great souvenirs and gifts. Group the finished candles together on a windowsill or table to make an attractive and colorful display.

1. Insert a length of primed wick into each wick holder and place a wick in the center of each tin.

2. In the top of a double boiler over medium heat, melt the stearin and wax dye, if using.

3. Add the wax. Melt and mix thoroughly. Heat to 190°F.

4. Anchor the wicks in the tins by pouring enough wax into each tin to cover about 1/2 inch of the wick. Allow the wax to cool for about 30 minutes.

5. Wrap the end of the wicks around tie rods and rest the rods on the tops of the containers. Take up any slack in the wicks and center them within the tins. Be careful not to dislodge the anchors.

6. Reheat the wax to 190°F and fill the tins to within 1/2 inch of the top. Allow to cool for one hour.

7. If the wax settles, reheat the remaining wax to 190°F and top off the candles as necessary.

8. Cool for several hours or overnight. Remove the tie rods, trim the wicks to 1/4 inch, and the candles are ready to light.

Four 6-inch lengths wire-core wick, primed

4 wick holders

4 tin cans, approximately 4-inches deep and 2-inches wide

2.5 ounces stearin

1 disk wax dye, if desired

1.5 pounds paraffin wax

over-dipped tapers

Over-dipping with another color completely changes the look of a candle, and it is a great way to hide mistakes. When the candle burns, the inner core is revealed; contrasting with the new outer color. The color you use for over-dipping needs to be much stronger than usual, since it must cover the wax beneath. Ordinarily you need four times as much dye for an over-dip as you would for a solid-colored candle.

1. In a 12-inch dipping can, set in the bottom of a double boiler over medium heat, melt the wax dye. Add the wax. Melt and mix thoroughly. Heat to 160°F.

2. Drape the candles' wick over 3 fingers so the candles hang evenly and separately. Dip them into the wax and hold for 3 seconds. Remove and hang the candles to dry.

3. To give the new coat a smooth clean finish, raise the wax temperature to 180°F. Dip the pair for another 3 seconds. Remove and allow the candles to cool completely.

4. Trim the wicks to ¼ inch before lighting.

15 disks wax dye

4 pounds dip-and-carve wax

1 pair Basic Recipe Dipped Candles, white

If you like, you can create a candle with two or more over-dips. After each over-dip, empty the dipping can and melt a new color and an additional four pounds wax. Allow the candle to cool completely between each new color, for at least two hours in a cool room, so the colors don't blend.

votive candles

Ordinary votive candles may be inexpensive and easily obtained, but there's nothing ordinary about these one hundred percent beeswax votives. They're a little taller than store-bought votives, and the beeswax makes them soft and aromatic. If you use candles to heat essential oils in a burner to release their fragrance, these are the votives for you. True votive molds are readily available and create a candle that is slightly narrower at the bottom than at the top. This pleasing profile is difficult to attain using found objects as molds—try tomato paste cans or small juice glasses. If you use found molds, you may need a little more beeswax than this recipe calls for.

Six 3-inch lengths wire-core wick

6 wick holders

0.5 pound beeswax

1. Prepare the molds—you will need 6 small votive molds. Insert the wicks into the wick holders and place one in each mold. Give each mold a spritz of silicon spray.

2. In the top of a double boiler over medium heat, melt the beeswax and heat to 160°F.

3. Transfer the wax to a pouring jug and fill the molds. Allow to cool overnight, then release the candles from the molds.

4. Trim the wicks to ¹/₄ inch, set in your favorite votive holders, and they are ready to light.

scented candles

After arriving home after a week or two away, lighting a scented candle is the fastest way to whisk away the musty smell houses often acquire when left empty. I prefer a spicy or citrus scent that's not too overpowering—something that's hard to find in a store-bought candle. By adapting the Basic Recipe Molded Candle, and adding a bit of candle scent or essential oil, you can create scented candles to your personal specifications.

1. Prepare the mold—you will need a 7 x 2-inch mold. Insert the primed wick in the mold: tie to a tie rod and seal with mold seal.

2. In the top of a double boiler over medium heat, melt the opaque crystals, then add the wax. Melt and mix thoroughly. Heat to 190°F.

3. Stir in the candle scent or essential oil and transfer the wax to a pouring jug. Carefully fill the mold and allow to cool for one hour.

4. Top off the candle as necessary, then leave to harden for 6 to 8 hours.

5. Unmold the candle, trim the wicks to ¼ inch, and level the candle bottom before lighting.

One 9-inch length wick, primed

1 tablespoon opaque crystals

0.5 pound paraffin wax

2 to 3 drops candle scent or essential oil

aromatherapy

Aromatherapy is based on the premise that fragrances can trigger an emotional reaction—smell pine and you may think of your childhood home at Christmas time; or smell a certain cologne and you might think of your husband. Those pleasant memories and aromas lift your spirits and help you relax. The essential oils used in aromatherapy also have therapeutic properties. Eucalyptus, for example, is good for clearing a stuffy nose, while rosemary will ease a headache, and lavender help an insomniac to fall asleep.

candy twists

These may look complicated and difficult to make, but they're actually quite easy. In fact, once you've dipped the candles, you're more than halfway there. The key is to work with the wax while it is still warm and pliable—use one pair of Basic Recipe Dipped Candles before they have time to harden. Bright colors are best for these candles. Add five squares of wax dye to the Basic Recipe and use dip-and-carve wax instead of beeswax (not paraffin, which is too brittle).

1. Cut the wick and separate the candles.

2. Place one of the candles on a smooth clean work surface. Use a rolling pin to flatten the candle to ¼-inch thick. Beginning about ½ inch above the base of the candle, gently roll it towards the top.

3. Holding the base of the candle in one hand and the tip in the other, turn the candle to create "twists." Make sure the twists are evenly distributed along the entire length of the candle.

4. Check the base to ensure it is still the right diameter for a candleholder and reshape if necessary.

5. Repeat steps 2 through 4 with the second candle.

6. Allow the candles to cool for at least 2 hours before trimming the wicks and lighting.

1 pair Basic Recipe Dipped Candles, colored and still warm

carved candles

This recipe takes over-dipping one step further: the original candle is over-dipped and then carved to reveal the base color. When lit, the candle glows through the design. Some very innovative patterns can be created—a steady hand and a bit of practice are all that's needed. You can use any sharp tool, such as a craft knife, scalpel, or awl to carve designs in the wax; but cutting tools, such as those used for making wood cuts, are the best. They're available at art supply stores in sets of different sizes and shapes.

1. In a 9-inch dipping can, set in the bottom of a double boiler over medium heat, melt the wax dye. Add the wax. Melt and mix thoroughly. Heat to 160°F.

2. Holding the candle carefully by the wick, dip it in the colored wax. Hold for 6 seconds, then remove and allow to cool for 2 hours, or until the outer layer is hardened.

3. Meanwhile, design the pattern you want to carve.

4. Use cutting tools to carve away the over-dip to reveal your design in the wax.

5. Trim the wick to ¼ inch and light.

12 disks wax dye

3 pounds dip-and-carve wax

1 Basic Recipe Molded Candle, white or cream

double dipping

Sometimes accidents produce amazing results. On a whim, I discovered the double-dip candle. I had dipped a candle but it turned out to be a shade of green I wasn't fond of. With my cutting tools, I carved a pattern through the green, revealing the white underneath. Then I dipped the candle in blue wax. This turned the white areas blue and the green areas a lovely teal. The combination was divine. Using two shades of the same color would be a variation.

1. In a 9-inch dipping can, set into the bottom of a double boiler over medium heat, melt the green wax dye. Add half the wax. Melt and mix thoroughly. Heat to 160°F.

2. Holding the candle carefully by the wick, dip it in the wax. Hold for 6 seconds, then remove and allow to cool for 2 hours, or until the outer layer is hardened.

3. Meanwhile, design the pattern you want to carve.

4. Use cutting tools to carve away the over-dip to reveal your design in the wax.

5. In the dipping can, set in the bottom of the double boiler over medium heat, melt the blue wax dye. Add the remaining wax. Melt and mix thoroughly. Heat to 160°F.

6. Holding the candle carefully by the wick, dip it in the wax. Hold for 6 seconds, then remove and allow to cool for 2 hours, or until the outer layer is hardened.

7. Trim the wick to 1/4 inch and light.

12 disks green wax dye

6 pounds dip-and-carve wax

1 Basic Recipe Molded Candle, white or cream

12 disks blue wax dye

bark candles

These wonderful, woodsy candles make excellent gifts. Beech and birch, both white and red, all work well and the effect, when you light these candles, is enchanting. These candles may test your carpentry skills; but they are well worth the effort. Use four votives from the recipe on page 43 (or substitute store-bought tea lights, if you prefer). You will also need a 1½-inch wood-boring bit.

1. Using a saw, cut the branch into 4 pieces of equal or varied lengths. To ensure that each length stands steadily, plane the bottom end of each until level.

2. Hold a branch piece steady by placing it vertically in a clamp or vice. With an electric drill and a 1½-inch wood-boring bit, drill a hole about 2 inches deep in the center of the branch end. Repeat this with the other 3 pieces.

3. Insert a votive candle, still in its mold, into each hole and the candles are ready to light.

One 2 x 16-inch branch

4 votive candles, with molds

The recipe here makes pillar-type candles, but you can work up variations, depending on the type of branch you use. For example, a branch with lots of nubs and knots might make a great horizontal candleholder for two or four tapers. A thicker bough might hold three votive candles, or tie three branches together in an attractive grouping. Take a walk in the woods, inspecting the branches and boughs you find along the way and see where your inspiration leads you!

tonal tapers

Here's a variation on the over-dipping technique that creates a new look for tapers. In this recipe, three shades of the same color are needed, and the resulting candles make a graceful addition to any dining table. Use Basic Recipe Dipped Candles for these tapers, but use dip-and-carve wax instead of beeswax to make the Basic Recipe candles.

1. In a 12-inch dipping can, set in the bottom of a double boiler over medium heat, melt 6 disks of the wax dye. Add the wax. Melt and mix thoroughly. Heat to 160°F. Turn the heat down to maintain the temperature if necessary.

2. Dip each pair of candles for 6 seconds.

3. Add another 6 disks of dye to the wax. Melt and mix thoroughly. Check that the wax temperature is 160°F. Dip the candles again—immersing them only two-thirds of the way. Hold for 6 seconds.

4. To add the final ring of color, add the last 6 disks of dye. Melt and mix thoroughly. Check that the wax temperature is 160°F. Dip the candles one-third of the way into the dipping can. Hold for 6 seconds.

6. Dry the candles overnight, then trim the wicks to 1/4 inch and light.

18 disks wax dye

4 pounds dip-and-carve wax

3 pairs Basic Recipe Dipped Candles, white

Instead of three shades of one color, try other color combinations—just dip the lightest color first. Depending on your color choices, you may need to empty your dipping can and refill it with another color wax. Be sure that your candle has cooled completely before dipping it in the new color, otherwise the colors will blend.

painted
candles

MAKES ONE 7 X 2-INCH PILLAR

Painting onto candles lets you turn plain molded candles (or even inexpensive store-bought candles) into personalized accents to your decor. The trick is to find poster or gouache paint (available in art supply and craft stores) that will actually stick to the shiny candle surface. Adding a drop or two of dish detergent to the paint will improve its adherence. (Also see page 89 for another method for painting candles.)

1. Plan your design.

2. Prepare the candle by wiping it clean and dry with an old nylon or chamois cloth. A rag dipped in paint or nail polish remover will remove most blemishes.

3. For each color, mix one teaspoon of paint with a pea-size drop of dish detergent. The paint should be thick, not runny.

4. Using an artist's paint brush, apply the paint to the candle. Swift brush strokes are the most effective.

5. Allow the paint to dry for about 30 minutes before handling or lighting the candle.

1 Basic Recipe Molded Candle

Gouache or poster paint in various colors

Instead of a paintbrush, use an old kitchen sponge or loofa to dab on the paint. This will produce a light, lacy look. You can also experiment with other applicators, such as a toothbrush, a balled up piece of fabric, and other household items.

stenciled candles

MAKES ONE 7 X 2-INCH PILLAR

With a cut-out stencil or paper doily, you can apply a pattern to candles. Stencils can be tricky, however, since the curve of the candle makes it difficult to keep the stencil flat against the surface, allowing paint to bleed underneath—so be sure to affix them firmly with tape. Small stencils work best since they lie flatter on the candle surface.

1. Wrap the stencil around the candle and tape firmly in place.

2. Mix one teaspoon of paint with a pea-size drop of dish detergent. (When painting with stencils, it's important to work with thick paint—you don't want the paint to run under the stencil!)

3. Using a fine-textured sponge or a small artist's paintbrush, apply the paint to the exposed areas of the candle. Paint the candle straight on, rather than at an angle, to avoid getting paint under the stencil.

4. To prevent smudging, allow the paint to dry with the stencil still in place for 2 hours, or until the paint is dry. Gently remove the stencil and the candle is ready to light.

1 paper stencil or doily

1 Basic Recipe Molded Candle

Gouache or poster paint

floating candles

You can buy floating-candle molds, or you can use any small mold you have around the house or in the kitchen—such as individual muffin or tart tins. Make a lovely centerpiece by floating two or three candles with a large flower blossom, or on their own, in a cut-glass bowl.

1. Prepare the molds—you will need 6 individual muffin or tart tins.

2. Insert a length of wick into each wick holder.

3. In the top of a double boiler over medium heat, melt the stearin and wax dye. Add the wax. Melt and mix thoroughly. Heat to 160°F.

4. To anchor the wicks, pour a small amount of wax into the molds, then insert a wick and wick holder into the middle of each. Allow the wax to cool for 5 minutes.

5. Reheat the wax to 160°F, then fill each mold to the top. Allow to cool completely, about one hour.

6. To remove the candles from their molds, simply tap the bottoms and pop out the candles. (If you have difficulty, put them in the refrigerator for 10 minutes, then try again.) Trim the wicks to ¹/₄ inch and float the candles in a bowl of water with some flowers.

Six 1.5 inch pieces thin, wire-core wick

6 wick holders

0.8 ounces stearin

1 disk wax dye

8 ounces paraffin wax

dried flower candles

MAKES ONE 7 X 2-INCH PILLAR

Embed flowers onto a candle by affixing dried flowers to the surface, then over-dipping in clear wax. This technique works especially well with interestingly shaped leaves and flat blooms. You can buy dried flowers, use plants from your garden, or wildflowers found in the fields—though fresh flowers need to be dried. Silicone beads (available in craft shops) quickly absorb moisture, but kitty litter is less expensive and works just as well.

1. If using fresh flowers, cover a cookie sheet with a layer of kitty litter and place the flowers and leaves on top. Sprinkle enough kitty litter over the flowers to completely cover. Leave to dry in a cool, dry place (where kitty can't get at them!) for at least a week. (Silicone beads work similarly, but will dry the flowers in 24 to 48 hours.)

2. Carefully remove the flowers from the litter and lay them out in a pleasing arrangement on a sheet of paper.

3. Use a dab of Stick-um™ to affix the flowers to the candle. Do this to each flower until the arrangement is complete, making sure the flowers remain flat against the candle.

4. In a 9-inch dipping can, set in the bottom of a double boiler over medium heat, melt the wax. Heat to 205°F. (Be extra vigilant at these temperatures.)

5. Holding the candle by the wick, carefully dip it in the wax. Hold for 5 seconds. Remove and make sure the flowers are flat.

6. Dip again for 5 seconds. Remove and leave to dry for 2 hours. Trim the wick to 1/4 inch and you are ready to light your candle.

2 pounds kitty litter

Fresh or dried flowers, such as pansies and violets

1 Basic Recipe Molded Candle

Stick-um™

1.5 pounds dip-and-carve or paraffin wax

ice candles

This is an excellent project for children ten years old and up—it is an interesting lesson in physics as it pertains to liquids and solids, and the contrast between hot and cold. These candles look their best in bold, primary colors—colors which appeal to children, too. A prepared taper forms the core of ice candles, so this is a great way to reuse candle stubs and less-than-successful homemade candles. You could also use store-bought tapers, if desired.

1. Prepare the mold—you will need a 1-quart milk carton. Cut away the top of the carton and discard. With a wicking needle, poke a hole in the center of the carton bottom.

2. Trim away the bottom 2 inches of the taper, exposing the wick. Thread the wick through the hole at the bottom of the carton, but don't knot it.

3. In the top of a double boiler over medium heat, melt the wax dye and wax. Mix thoroughly and heat to 200°F.

4. While the wax is melting, break the ice cubes into $1/2$- to $3/4$-inch irregular chunks. (Store-bought ice cubes, which usually have holes in them, break more easily and provide more interesting results.)

5. Arrange the ice chunks around the taper in the carton. The ice will prop up the taper so it stands upright. Put the carton in a cake pan or other flat-bottomed pan with high sides.

6. Carefully pour the wax in a circular fashion around the taper; this will prevent the ice from melting unevenly. Fill the carton to the top with the wax.

7. As the ice melts, water will leak out of the mold through the wick

One 10-inch taper

2 disks wax dye

1 pound paraffin wax

1 quart ice cubes

hole at the bottom. Allow to cool for 2 hours, during which time the ice will melt completely.

8. Pour off any water remaining in the mold, then peel away the carton to reveal the candle. Gently shake the candle to dislodge any lingering water droplets.

9. Allow the candle to dry completely, for at least two days, before you trim the wick to ¼ inch and light.

variations

For this recipe, a quart-size milk carton about 8 inches tall is used, but you could use a carton or container of any size; just keep in mind that plastic-coated paper works best. You can cut the mold so that it is 8 inches tall (as here) or just 2 inches tall. This recipe easily adapts to any size of taper or stub and the type of carton. To figure out how much wax you'll need, use the guidelines in Chapter One (3 ounces wax to every 3.5 ounces water needed to fill the container). You probably won't need quite so much, however, since the ice and the prepared taper will take up a good portion of that space. It's hard to predict exactly how much less you'll need, and it's better to err on the side of too much rather than too little.

cookie-cutter candles

This is another way to take hum-drum candles and make them more fun and colorful. Small cookie cutters and fat, white candles work best here. The shapes adhere well to the candle and are easy to mold because of their high beeswax content.

1. Line a cookie sheet with waxed paper and set aside.

2. In the top of a double boiler over medium heat, melt the wax dye, beeswax, and paraffin wax. Mix thoroughly and heat to 150°F. Pour the wax onto the prepared cookie sheet to form a layer no more than 1/8-inch deep. Allow to harden for about 10 minutes.

3. Using cookie cutters, cut shapes out of the wax. Make sure the cutter goes all the way through the wax. Allow the wax to continue to harden for another 10 minutes.

4. Invert the cookie sheet onto a clean surface and peel away the waxed paper. Separate the shapes from the surrounding wax.

5. One by one, take the shapes and hold them against the candles, molding them to fit the candles' curvature. (You may need to soften the shapes slightly with a hairdryer.)

6. Dab Stick-um™ on the back of each shape and carefully press the shapes onto the candles. Trim the wicks to 1/4 inch and the candles are ready to light.

1 disk wax dye

0.5 pound beeswax

0.5 pound paraffin wax

2 Basic Recipe Molded Candles

Stick-um™

Use your handmade candles as decorative accents to your home, as here where dipped and molded candles artfully lean against a chimney flue, as if placed by accident. In fact, the colors were carefully dyed to match the colors in the room and harmonize with the wonderful mustard-painted wall.

chapter three

Sitting on the porch, listening to the crickets chirruping and watching the sun go down, or celebrating with friends in the backyard on a summer evening, is much more special when candles provide the only light. Candlelight lends just the right illumination without disturbing the mystery of darkness. Outdoor electricity has its uses, but not if you want your outside space to be taken out of the realm of the ordinary.

Mostly, we associate candles outside with summertime barbecues—but there's a place for outdoor candles in every season. With their warmth and lustrous light, candles make the outdoors welcoming at any time of the year.

Imagine a pond-side party on a moonlit night in late fall. The guests arrive at sunset and follow luminaria along a path through the fields, to a blazing bonfire set beside the water. After a delicious dinner, served buffet-style from a farm wagon, an old-time fiddler takes requests. And as the darkness falls, the fire, the candles, and the moon shed their glowing light and create an intimate space in the middle of an open field.

This is the magic of candles outdoors.

sand candles

MAKES ONE 3 X 5-INCH CANDLE

This is the quintessential summertime candle. Use several in different colors and sizes to light a beach party or to remind you of the beach when you're in the yard or on the porch. (The photograph at the beginning of this chapter shows sand candles lined up on a piece of driftwood at the seashore.)

1. In a large bowl (at least 6 x 12-inches), mix the sand with the water. Stir thoroughly to ensure the water is evenly distributed.

2. Using the heel of your hand, firmly pack the sand down into the bowl.

3. To make the sand mold, use a smaller bowl (or any smaller spherical shape), to make an impression in the sand about $2\frac{1}{2}$ x 5 inches. Press any sand that pushes up and around the bowl back down to make a smooth, firm edge. Gently remove the bowl.

4. In a medium-size saucepan over medium heat, melt the stearin and wax dye. Melt and mix thoroughly.

5. Add the wax. Melt and mix thoroughly. Heat to 260°F.

6. Holding a metal spoon in one hand and the saucepan in the other, trickle the wax onto the back of the spoon and into the sand mold. The spoon will slow the flow of hot wax and help prevent splashing. (You can't totally prevent splashing, but a bit of wax on the outside of the mold won't affect the final result—just take care not to burn yourself. Wear oven mitts on both hands.) Fill the mold halfway, then wait for 5 minutes to allow the wax to seep into the sand. Return the wax to the heat and maintain 260°F.

10 pounds fine sand

2 cups water

0.5 ounce stearin

1 disk wax dye, if desired

0.5 pound paraffin wax

One 5-inch length medium wire-core wick, primed

7. Fill the rest of the mold with wax, then allow the candle to cool for 2 hours.

8. During cooling, a well will form in the center of the candle. Reheat the wax to 260°F and top up the mold. Leave the candle to cool for another 2 hours, until the wax is firm but not completely hard.

9. To wick the candle, push a wicking needle into the middle of the candle to make a $2^1/_2$-inch-deep hole. Insert the wick into the hole and allow the candle to harden for 3 hours longer.

10. Gently lift the candle out of the bowl, brushing away any excess sand. The candle may have a few jagged edges or irregularities where the wax has seeped unevenly. Use a vegetable peeler and sandpaper to peel and rub away bumps and imperfections.

11. To make a flat base for the candle, warm a large saucepan, set the candle inside, and gently rotate for 5 seconds. Remove the candle and leave to cool overnight. Once you've trimmed the wick to $^1/_4$ inch, you're ready for your beach party.

To make sand candles, the wax needs to seep into the sand. To accomplish this, the wax is heated to 260°F—much hotter than can be reached using a double boiler. For this reason, the wax is heated directly over the heat source. Monitor the wax temperature very carefully so that it doesn't overheat and catch fire—wax will combust at about 375°F. (Check the section on safety on page 25.) Do not attempt to use this recipe unless you have a thermometer that reads temperatures up to 275°F. Guess work can be dangerous.

beehive candle

What could be more appropriate than making a beehive candle out of beeswax sheets? These sturdy, stately candles look fabulous on a screened porch or backyard patio.

Four 8 x 16-inch beeswax sheets

One 10-inch length #3 square-braided wick

1. Place the beeswax sheets, side by side, on a work surface with the long sides nearest you. Using a straightedge as a guide and a craft knife, cut the first sheet on a diagonal, beginning at the top left-hand corner and ending one inch down from the top right-hand corner.

2. Cut the second sheet on a diagonal, beginning one inch below the top left-hand corner and ending 2 inches down from the top right-hand corner.

3. Cut the third sheet on a diagonal, beginning 2 inches below the top left-hand corner and ending 3 inches down from the top right-hand corner.

4. Cut the fourth sheet on a diagonal, beginning 3 inches below the top left-hand corner and ending 4 inches down from the top right-hand corner.

5. Carefully remove the top shapes from each of the cut sheets and reserve—you'll use these portions in reverse size order when you make the second half of the candle.

6. You now need to link the wax sheets together. Match up the short sides of the wax sheets that are the same length. (You may not have room to link all the sheets at one time.) Placing the sheets side by side, press the wax edges together to begin to form a long triangle. If necessary, use a hairdryer to soften the wax.

7. Press the wick along the 8-inch edge of the first sheet. One inch of wick should extend beyond each side.

8. Start rolling the candle, taking care to keep the edges even along the bottom edge. To achieve a tighter roll, insert a piece of waxed paper between your fingers and the wax.

9. When you have rolled all but the last 6 inches of the first series of linked sheets of wax, link one or two more sheets by pressing the same-sized edges together. Continue linking and rolling until all the wax sheets are used, including the reserved portions.

10. Press the edge of the wax into the candle to seal, softening the wax with a hairdryer if necessary.

11. Prime and trim the wick to $\frac{1}{4}$ inch, and your beehive candle is ready to light.

citronella-scented flowerpot candles

Here's a great way to keep bugs at bay on a patio or rocking-chair porch. Clay or terra-cotta flowerpots will look adorable, but you could also use tiny galvanized buckets or other garden containers. When you're shopping for pots, compare the size of the drainage holes. Since you need to seal these up, the smaller the better. Of course, you can use beeswax for these candles, but if their primary purpose is utilitarian, paraffin is just as good.

1. Prepare the flowerpots. Seal the hole at the bottom of the pots with a hunk of mold seal and secure with a strip of masking tape.

2. Insert the wicks into the wick holders and place one in the center of each pot.

3. In the top of a double boiler over medium heat, melt the stearin and wax. Heat to 160°F. Add the citronella essential oil and stir thoroughly.

4. To anchor the wicks, pour a small amount of wax into each pot. Allow the wax to harden for 10 minutes.

5. Reheat the remaining wax to 160°F and fill the pots to the desired height—about one inch from the top works well. (It will prevent a breeze from blowing out the flame.) Allow to cool and harden overnight.

6. Trim the wicks to ¼ inch and light.

Four 4-inch flowerpots

Four 6-inch lengths medium wire-core wick

4 wick holders

1.5 ounces stearin

1 pound paraffin wax

2 ounces citronella essential oil

If you feel like taking this delightful recipe one step further, tie lengths of wire around the flowerpots and make a loop for a handle. Then you can suspend your citronella candles from hooks and branches.

iceberg candles

These easy-to-make candles will beautifully light any evening-time celebration. They look like little icebergs—hence their name! They are particularly effective when displayed on a mirror, as shown here, and used as a centerpiece for your table.

1. Using a hammer and chisel, break the block of wax into 5 irregular shapes—each about 5 inches tall and 4 inches wide. Just a gentle tap will break off a chunk. Make sure that at least one side of each shape is flat so the candle will stand sturdily.

2. To wick the candles, hold them steady by placing each block, flat side down, in a clamp. With an 8-inch, $1/16$th drill bit, drill a hole down through the center of each block.

3. Thread a wick through each of the drilled holes. If necessary, use a wicking needle. Tie a knot at the bottom end of each wick, leaving about 3 extra inches at the top.

4. In a dipping can large enough to take the largest block, set in the bottom of a double boiler over medium heat, melt the remaining $1^1/2$ pounds of wax. Heat to 160°F.

5. Holding each iceberg by its wick, dip into the wax. Hold for 10 seconds. Remove and allow the candles to dry for one hour.

6. Trim the wicks, top and bottom, before arranging and lighting.

One 10-pound block plus 1.5 pounds paraffin wax

Five 7-inch lengths wire-core wick, primed

Wax is brittle and prone to cracking, so one or two of the shapes may break during drilling. Either use the pieces to make smaller icebergs, or patch them back together with a little of the melted wax. If you decide that you can't rescue the pieces, add them to the wax you'll be using to over-dip the surviving icebergs.

luminaria

Luminaria provide easy and effective lighting for an outdoor party. They're especially good for illuminating a path to a party tent. Usually paper bags are used to make luminaria, but if you feel like a variation, why not try using another type of bag? Foil bags (which are really inside-out coffee bags) provide a lovely reflective surface and are reminiscent of the hole-punch metal lanterns of earlier days. They are also sturdier than paper bags and have the added advantage of being fireproof!

1. Turn the bags inside out and wash thoroughly.

2. Flatten out the bags, and using a small pair of scissors, a craft knife, or a hole puncher, cut out pleasing patterns for the candlelight to shine through. You can either cut out an attractive mirror image, or place a piece of sturdy card inside the bag so you only cut through one side at a time.

3. Fill the bottom of each bag with 2 cups of the sand and stand one votive in the center of each.

4. Set the luminaria on a patio table, around a spa, or on a deck railing, and light the night!

6 foil bags

12 cups sand

6 votive candles (see page 43)

large floating candles

All candles float since wax is lighter than water, but in order for a candle to float upright (and therefore stay lit), it must be wider than it is tall. It's also best if the top is wider than the bottom—like a pie plate. These large candles are wonderful for floating in a pond, swimming pool, or water garden—try dyeing them green so they look like lily pads. Adding beeswax to the mix extends burning time and softens the green coloring so they look even more natural.

1. Prepare the mold—you will need an 8-inch pie plate. Spritz with silicone spray.

2. Insert the wicks into the wick holders and arrange them, equally spaced, in the pie plate.

3. In the top of a double boiler over a medium heat, melt the stearin and wax dye. Add the paraffin wax and beeswax. Melt and mix thoroughly. Heat to 160°F.

4. Anchor the wicks by pouring wax to a depth of 1/3 inch into the pie plate. Allow to cool for 10 minutes.

5. Reheat the wax to 160°F and fill the mold to the top. Allow to cool for one hour.

6. If the wax settles during cooling, reheat the remaining wax to 160°F, and top off the candle. Allow to cool. You may have to repeat this process 2 or 3 times to achieve a level surface.

7. Cool for several hours or overnight, then release the candle from the mold and trim the wicks to 1/4 inch. Light and float.

Three 2-inch lengths medium wire-core wick, primed

3 wick holders

3.2 ounces stearin

3 disks wax dye

1 pound paraffin wax

0.5 pound beeswax

torches

Handmade torches are a great way to light up any outdoor party; they provide glorious illumination and they look wonderful made with colored wax—in fact, the brighter the better. You can make them in a variety of sizes, like the smaller ones shown opposite.

1. Line 2 cookie sheets with waxed paper.

2. In the top of a double boiler over medium heat, melt the beeswax. Heat to 160°F. Add the citronella essential oil and mix thoroughly.

3. Pour the wax in a thin layer onto the prepared cookie sheets and allow to cool for 30 minutes.

4. Lift the wax and waxed paper from one of the cookie sheets. Invert onto a clean, dry surface and peel off the waxed paper.

5. Position the wax sheet with a long side nearest you. Press a length of wick along the long edge nearest you so 2 inches extends beyond what will eventually be the top of the candle. Place the bamboo stake along the same edge so the top of the stake is about 1/4 inch below the end of the wick, and extending about 18 inches below what will be the bottom of the candle. (Only the bottom 5 or so inches of the candle will wrap around the stake.)

6. Begin rolling the wax around the wick and stake. Use a piece of waxed paper to achieve a tight roll.

7. When the candle is completely rolled, squeeze the candle to fuse the layers together and secure it to the stake.

8. Repeat steps 4 through 7 with the second wax sheet.

9. Prime the wicks and allow to dry overnight.

10. Trim the wicks to 1/4 inch before lighting your torches.

1.5 pounds beeswax

2 tablespoons citronella essential oil

Two 12-inch lengths #1 square wick

Two 24 x 0.5-inch garden bamboo stakes or other sticks

candles in seashells

MAKES SIX CANDLES

If you're like most people, you can't resist picking up seashells on the beach. Now you have a good reason to take them home. Lovely on their own, or as splendid companions to sand candles, candles in seashells celebrate the beach and the summer. Collect only good-sized empty shells, or save the shells from your next clambake or oyster fest.

1. Clean the seashells thoroughly. Then, to be sure they are really clean, put them in boiling water for a few minutes.

2. Insert the wicks into the wick holders and place one in the middle of each seashell.

3. In the top of a double boiler over medium heat, melt the stearin and wax dye, if using. Add the wax. Melt and mix thoroughly. Heat to 160°F.

4. Fill each seashell nearly to the top and allow to cool completely, or overnight.

5. Trim the wicks to ¼ inch and arrange the candles on a dish or in a bowl of sand. Light and enjoy!

1.5 x 6.5-inch seashells

Six 2-inch lengths thin wire wick, primed

6 wick holders

0.8 ounces stearin

1 disk wax dye, if desired

8 ounces paraffin wax

ice lanterns

Ice lanterns break the long, cold darkness of winter with a golden glow. Place one or two outside the front door, or make several and line a walkway. They are the perfect way to welcome guests to a winter dinner party. You can also add flowers, herbs, or other botanicals to the water and freeze it in layers, or color the water with food dye.

One good handful sand or small weight

1 votive (see page 43)

1. Prepare the molds—you will need one freezer-proof bucket or bowl, about 7 x 8 inches, and one freezer-proof bowl, about 5 x 4 inches.

2. Fill the large container with water to 2 inches from the top.

3. Take the small container and fill with water. Add the sand or small weight and push the container into the large container—immersing it about 4 inches and centering carefully. Crisscross tape across the containers to hold the small container securely in place.

4. Put into the freezer and leave for 24 hours, or until frozen solid.

5. To unmold the lantern, remove the tape and fill the kitchen sink or a large basin with hot water. Put the mold into the water. This will release the lantern from both containers.

6. Put the ice lantern on your doorstep and place a lit votive in the indent left by the smaller container. Light the way to your door and welcome your guests!

If the outside temperature is above freezing, place the unmolded lantern in the freezer until just before your guests are due to arrive. Even in warmer weather, these lanterns will last at least two or three hours. At below freezing they will last indefinitely, and you can store them for as long as you like in the freezer.

chapter four

candles for special occasions

Sometimes the most successful dinner parties are those where friends gather and prepare the meal together. Working closely helps foster a cooperative spirit, and the creativity involved makes the whole process a relaxing kind of fellowship.

The recipes in this chapter can work in the same way. Families or friends can take on these projects in anticipation and preparation for a special occasion or holiday. Before a wedding, friends of the bride and groom might gather to create wedding-cake candles for table centerpieces. Making candles in eggshells is a welcome change to the family tradition of coloring eggs before Easter. In preparation for a Fourth of July party, a relaxing day spent decorating candles is a wonderful way to begin the summer season. And what could be more fun, on a blustery fall day, than to pick out seasonal vegetables at the farmers' market, and turning them into floating-candle centerpieces when you get home?

Many of the projects in this chapter can involve children—what better way to explain and help them appreciate a holiday and its meaning? Making candles for these special moments could become one of your family's traditions!

candles in eggshells

MAKES SIX CANDLES

You'll be making omelets for dinner after creating these delightful candles. Arranged as a centerpiece or displayed in eggcups at each place setting, these candles are perfect for Easter or other springtime celebration. Use extra-large white or brown eggs, and either leave them in their natural state, or experiment with dying or painting the eggshells.

1. Using a small knife, gently tap the smaller end of each egg. Break off the top quarter of the shell, removing a small amount at first. Then carefully remove additional pieces to make a jagged edge. Pour the raw eggs into a bowl.

2. To remove the skin from inside the shell, use tweezers to puncture the bubble at the bottom. Gently rub the inside of the shell with your finger, rolling the skin up as you rub.

3. Insert the wicks into the wick holders and place one inside each eggshell. Place the eggshells in an egg carton.

4. In the top of a double boiler over medium heat, melt the wax dye, if using, and the wax. Mix thoroughly and heat to 160°F.

5. To anchor the wicks, pour a little wax into each eggshell. Allow the wax to harden for 15 minutes.

6. Reheat the wax to 160°F. Fill the eggshells with an equal amount of wax—to the height of the lowest eggshell edge. Allow the candles to cool and harden overnight.

7. Arrange in eggcups, trim the wicks to ¼ inch, and light.

6 eggs

Six 2-inch lengths thin wire wick, primed

6 wick holders

1 disk yellow wax dye, if desired

0.5 pound beeswax or paraffin wax

wedding-cake candle

A very special day calls for a very special candle, and this wedding-cake candle is just that! You can make this candle using commercially available molds or by finding tin cans of the correct size. For example, you could use various sized tuna cans: a family-size can would make a great base. An eight-ounce can could form the middle tier, with a three-ounce can on top. There's just one problem with this candle—it's so beautiful, you may never want to light it!

1. Prepare the molds—you will need one $3^1/_2$ x 4-inch mold, one 2 x 3-inch mold, and one $1^1/_2$ x 2-inch mold.

2. In the top of a double boiler over medium heat, melt the opaque crystals and 1 pound of the wax. Mix thoroughly and heat to 170°F.

3. Pour the wax into the unwicked molds and allow to cool for 6 hours or overnight.

4. Release the wax from the molds. Use Stick-um™ to affix the medium-size candle to the top of the large candle. Affix the small candle on top of the medium-size one, making sure each one is centered atop the other.

5. Using an 8-inch $^1/_{16}$th drill bit, drill a hole through the center of the stacked candles. (Alternatively, drill each candle separately before you stack them. Just be sure you hit the exact center of each candle, or else your wedding cake will be off balance. Use a wicking needle to check that the holes line up.)

6. To wick the candle, thread a wicking needle with the wick to pull it through the hole. Use a wick holder to anchor the bottom.

2 tablespoons opaque crystals

5 pounds paraffin wax

Stick-um™

9-inch length medium to wide wire-core wick, primed

1 wick holder

Fake pearls

Dried flowers (feverfew, statis, or baby's breath)

0.8-inch-wide length of ribbon

7. In a 12-inch dipping can, set in the bottom of the double boiler over medium heat, melt the remaining wax. Heat to 190°F.

8. Holding the candle by its wick, dip it in the wax for 5 seconds. Remove and allow to cool for 5 minutes.

8. To decorate the cake, arrange the fake pearls between the tiers to hide the joins between the candle. Attach flowers, leaves, and ribbons using Stick-um™ to hold them in place.

9. Trim the wick to ¼ inch, sit back, and admire your creation.

painted
independence day candles

MAKES TWO 7 X 2-INCH PILLARS

Independence Day is an occasion that calls for something extra special, and these candles fit the bill. Although a little more difficult to work with than poster paint or gouache, wax paint has better adherence, and also creates brighter colors—just right for a red, white, and blue July 4th–theme. To achieve the best effects you need to use quick, even strokes of paint, but that's a style that lends itself to Independence Day motifs, such as stripes and fireworks.

1. Carefully plan your designs. On one candle make a pattern of red and blue stripes, for example. On the other candle create a red and blue fireworks design.

2. Put 2 tablespoons of the wax and the blue wax dye into an individual muffin or tart tin. In another tin, place the other 2 tablespoons wax and the red dye. Fill a saucepan with about ½ inch water and place the muffin tins in the saucepan. Over medium-low heat, melt the wax dye and wax, mixing thoroughly.

3. Dip a soft artist's paintbrush into the melted wax. Apply your design to the candles using quick, even strokes. Use a different paintbrush for each color, or apply the blue paint on both candles first, then clean the brush thoroughly and apply the red. Dip the brush frequently because the wax hardens quickly. Leave the brush in the wax for 20 seconds each time you dip, so any old wax on the brush will be re-melted.

4. When the designs are complete, allow the candles to dry for one hour. Trim the wicks to ¼ inch before lighting.

4 tablespoons beeswax or paraffin wax

2 disks blue wax dye

2 disks red wax dye

2 Basic Recipe Molded Candles, white

stars-&-stripes candles

MAKES FOUR 7 X 2-INCH PILLARS

This is a simple variation on the Cookie-Cutter Candle on page 62. Instead of making your own sheets of wax, this recipe uses colored beeswax sheets to make these enchanting Fourth of July pillars. This is a perfect project for children—it doesn't use hot wax, there are very few sharp edges, and the results are bright and colorful. Star-shaped cookie cutters work well here; otherwise, cut stars out freehand, or trace a paper pattern.

1. Place the beeswax sheets on a clean work surface and use star-shaped cookie cutters and a craft knife to cut out star shapes and stripes. Lift up and remove the excess wax surrounding the stars and stripes.

2. Place a dab of Stick-um™ on each point of the stars, and at either end and in the middle of the stripes. Carefully press the shapes onto the pillar candles. Use a hairdryer to make the beeswax more pliable and to bring out its natural stickiness.

3. Trim the wicks to ¼ inch, light your candles, and enjoy!

**One 8 x 16-inch
sheet red beeswax**

**One 8 x 16-inch
sheet blue beeswax**

Stick-um™

**4 Basic Recipe Molded Candles,
white**

jack-o'-lantern candles

Create very special jack-o'-lanterns by over-dipping a round candle with orange wax, then use woodcutting tools to carve out the face. Make several and place them on windowsills on Halloween night or at each table setting at a Halloween dinner party. This is a great project to do with kids—just instruct them to be careful when handling the sharp instruments. Adapt the recipe for Luminaria on page 74 and accompany your jack-o'-lanterns with spooky luminaria!

1. Prepare and wick the molds—you will need four 2½-inch round molds.

2. In the top of a double boiler over medium heat, melt the opaque crystals and paraffin wax. Mix thoroughly and heat to 170°F.

3. Transfer the wax to a pouring jug and carefully fill the molds. Allow to cool for 2 hours, then release the candles from the molds.

4. In the top of the double boiler over medium heat, melt the stearin and wax dye. Add the dip-and-carve wax. Melt and mix thoroughly. Heat to 170°F.

5. Dip each of the candles into the wax for 5 seconds. Remove and allow to cool for at least 2 hours.

6. While the candles are cooling, plan your pumpkin faces. Keep them simple—curved lines can be tricky to carve without chipping away extra wax. (Sharp tools are the key to successful and precise carving.)

7. Carve out the pumpkin faces to reveal the white candle beneath the orange skin.

8. Trim the wicks to ¼ inch and light your Halloween celebration!

Four 4-inch lengths 2/0 wick

2 tablespoons opaque crystals

2 pounds paraffin wax

1 ounce stearin

15 disks orange wax dye

0.75 pound dip-and-carve wax

floating gourd & pumpkin candles

MAKES SIX FLOATING CANDLES

What a fun and easy decoration for Halloween or Thanksgiving! Miniature pumpkins and small gourds are often on sale at farmers' markets in the fall, and they make perfect little holders for the votives on page 43. Choose three orange gourds (Jack-be-Little is a common variety) and three white gourds (called Baby Boo) and float the candles in a large bowl or bucket.

1. Fill a large bowl or bucket with water and test each vegetable for floatability. Ideally, each should be able to float upright with its stem pointing upwards.

2. Carve a hole in each vegetable for the votives, removing the stem in the process. The hole should be $1\frac{1}{2}$ inch in diameter and about 2-inches deep. Insert a votive into each hole—the votives should fit securely, but you shouldn't have to force them.

3. Before you light the candles, test-float each vegetable to make sure they will still float upright. (Carving a deeper hole sometimes helps vegetables become more seaworthy.)

4. Arrange in a large bowl or bucket and light.

6 gourds or small pumpkins

6 votives

Once you get going on this idea for floating vegetables, it's easy to get carried away—try little patty-pan squash, apples, melons, and other fruits and vegetables. Most of them will float and will form the basis for interesting and original centerpieces for your dining table in any season.

fluted candles

Before heading to the recycling center with your old tin cans and corrugated cardboard, put them to good use and create these rusticated pillar candles. Some people call these embossed candles because the imprint of the corrugated cardboard shapes the candle. But the end result really looks like fluted columns.

1. Prepare the mold—you will need one 5 x 2-inch tin can. If possible, choose a can with smooth sides; this helps to slide the candle out more easily when it's time to unmold. Also, look for one that can be opened at both ends with a can opener.

2. Use an awl to make a hole in the center of the can bottom. (Presumably, you've already removed the top and used the contents.)

3. Cut out an 8 x 6-inch strip of corrugated cardboard to line the inside of the can. The cardboard ridges should point inward and vertically. Spray the corrugated (ridged) side of the cardboard with silicone spray. On the outside (smooth side) of the cardboard, join the seam with a piece of masking tape.

4. Tie a knot at one end of the wick and thread the wick through the hole in the bottom of the can. Wrap the end of the wick around a tie rod; rest the rod on top of the can and pull the wick taut, making sure that it is centered. Seal the hole at the bottom with mold seal.

5. In the top of a double boiler over medium heat, melt the stearin and wax dye. Add the wax. Melt and mix thoroughly. Heat to 180°F.

6. Anchor the wick by pouring about ¼ inch of wax into the bottom of the mold. Allow the wax to cool for 30 minutes.

One 8-inch length #1 wick, primed

2.5 ounces stearin

1 disk wax dye, or more as desired

1.5 pounds paraffin wax

7. Reheat the wax to 180°F, then fill the mold to the top with wax. Allow to cool for one hour.

8. If the wax settles, top off the candle with the remaining wax. If necessary repeat the process 2 or 3 times to achieve a level surface.

9. Cool the candle for 6 hours or overnight. Cut the knot that anchors the wick at the bottom of the can and use a can opener to remove the bottom of the can.

10. Fill a large saucepan with enough water to immerse the mold and bring to a boil. Holding the candle by the wick, carefully dip the candle and mold into the boiling water. Hold for 6 seconds (just long enough to heat the outer layer of wax). The cardboard and candle should now slide easily out of the can. (The can will be hot, so wear gloves to protect your hands.) If it doesn't slide out easily, dip the candle in the hot water again.

11. Gently peel the cardboard away from the candle, then trim the wick and you're done.

There's no way around it, removing the cardboard from a fluted candle is a slow process. To make it easier, either dampen the cardboard with water or use a silicone spray before filling the mold with wax. Nevertheless, it takes a bit of patience to remove the cardboard from the candle; carefully peeling it away and prying it out from the flutes with an awl. But the end results are well worth the time and effort. In any event, the appearance of the candle with a bit of paper embedded in the surface is very attractive, especially when the candle has been dyed a dark color such as cranberry.

primitive spiced tapers

These spice-coated candles are perfect for the holiday season. They make an elegant and original centerpiece for a dining table or an unusual mantle display. Use your favorite ground spices here: cumin, cinnamon, nutmeg, paprika, or others. As the candles burn, their scent will combine with the fragrance of the beeswax, creating a delicious and enticing aroma in the room.

1. Line 2 cookie sheets with waxed paper.

2. In the top of a double boiler over medium heat, melt the beeswax. Heat to 160°F.

3. Pour half of the wax onto each prepared cookie sheet in a thin layer about ⅛-inch thick. Allow to cool for 30 minutes.

4. Lift the waxed paper along with the wax from one of the cookie sheets. Invert the wax onto a clean, dry surface and peel away the waxed paper.

5. Working quickly, press a length of wick into one of the shorter sides of the wax sheet. The wick should be at least 2 inches longer than the wax sheet. Start to roll the wax around the wick, taking care to keep the edges even. Keep a piece of waxed paper between your fingers and the wax to achieve a tight roll. When it is completely rolled, squeeze the candle to fuse the layers together.

6. Repeat steps 4 and 5 with the second wax sheet.

7. In a 12-inch dipping can, set in the bottom of the double boiler over medium heat, melt the dip-and-carve wax. Heat to 160°F.

8. While the wax is melting, spread the spice on a clean cookie sheet in an even layer.

1 pound beeswax

Two 11-inch lengths square wick

4 pounds dip-and-carve wax

1 cup ground spice

9. Holding the candles by their wick, carefully dip them into the wax. Hold for 3 seconds. Remove and allow to cool for 3 minutes, or until the wax has cooled slightly but is still tacky.

10. Roll the candles in the spice until they are completely coated.

11. Prime the wicks, then leave the candles to cool and dry overnight.

12. Trim the wicks to $1/4$ inch and the candles are ready to light.

primitive herb-flecked candles

MAKES EIGHT 5-INCH CANDLES

Combining the natural allure of beeswax with favorite herbs creates candles that are simplicity itself—they never fail to intrigue and delight. Make them for really special occasions, such as Christmas. Because you make the sheets of beeswax yourself, and use the heat of your hands to roll and mold the candles, their appearance is much as candles might have looked in earlier times.

1. Line two cookie sheets with waxed paper.

2. In the top of a double boiler over medium heat, melt the beeswax. Heat to 160°F and stir in the herbs.

3. Pour half the wax onto each prepared cookie sheets in a thin layer about ⅛-inch thick. Allow to cool for 30 minutes.

4. Lift the waxed paper along with the wax from one of the cookie sheets. Invert onto a clean, dry surface and peel away the waxed paper. Cut the wax sheet into quarters and separate the sheets.

5. Working quickly, press a length of wick into one of the shorter sides of one of the wax sheets. The wick should be at least 2 inches longer than the wax sheet. Start to roll the wax around the wick, taking care to keep the edges even. Keep a piece of waxed paper between your fingers and the wax to achieve a tight roll. When it is completely rolled up, squeeze the candle to fuse the layers together.

6. Repeat steps 4 and 5 with the 3 remaining quarters and then with the second wax sheet.

7. Prime the wicks, then leave the candles to cool and dry overnight. Trim the wicks to ¼ inch before lighting.

1 pound beeswax

0.25 cup dried herbs (thyme, parsley, sage, rosemary, or tarragon)

Eight 7-inch lengths square wick

spice-encrusted candles

Make lots of these candles—in colors such as red, harvest gold, and forest green—in time for late fall and the winter holidays. Grouping two or three with some evergreen boughs, or next to a cornucopia, creates a beautiful centerpiece, side-table display, or original mantle arrangement.

1. Prepare and wick the mold—you will need one 2½-inch round mold.

2. In the top of a double boiler over medium heat, melt the stearin and wax dye. Add the wax. Melt and mix thoroughly. Heat to 170°F.

3. Carefully pour enough wax into the mold to fill it completely. Transfer the unused wax to a dipping can large enough to dip the candle. Allow the candle to cool for 3 hours, then release it from the mold.

4. Set the dipping can into the bottom of the double boiler and, over a medium heat, remelt the wax. Heat to 150°F.

5. While the wax is melting, put the chili seeds on a flat plate or into a pie plate.

6. Dip the candle into the wax and hold for 3 seconds. Remove and allow the candle to cool for 3 minutes, or until the wax has cooled but is still tacky.

7. Roll the candle in the chili seeds until completely coated. Leave the candle to cool for 2 hours.

8. Prime the wick and allow the candle to cool for 2 hours, or until it is completely dry.

9. Trim the wick to ¼ inch before lighting.

4 inch length 2/0 wick

0.8 ounces stearin

1 disk wax dye

1 pound dip-and-carve wax

0.5 cup dried chili seeds

decoupage candles

MAKES ONE 7 X 2-INCH PILLAR

With decoupage candles, you can display last year's Christmas cards at this year's celebration instead of storing them in a box in the attic! Family photographs and greeting cards alike make great images for these candles. Just be sure there's no printing on the back of the picture—because it will show through once the candle's been over-dipped.

1. Using small, sharp scissors or a craft knife, carefully cut out the image from the greeting card or photograph. Try to avoid sharp edges and overly complicated cutouts because the edges may peel away from the curve of the candle.

2. Use Stick-um™ to affix the image to the candle. Placing a sheet of waxed paper between the image and your fingers will prevent smudging.

3. In a 9-inch dipping can, set in the bottom of a double boiler over medium heat, melt the wax. Heat to 180°F.

4. Holding the candle by the wick, dip for 5 seconds, then remove.

5. Using the waxed paper, press the image onto the candle to ensure it has properly adhered.

6. If desired, dip the candle a second time for another 5 seconds, but remember that the additional wax will begin to blur your image.

7. Allow the candle to cool overnight.

8. Trim the wick to 1/4 inch and light. (Take particular care when burning candles with paper decorations.)

1 greeting card or photograph

Stick-um™

1 Basic Recipe Molded Candle

1 pound paraffin wax

wrapped candles

By now you may have found that not all your forays into candle-making have been as successful as you might have wished. Even the most experienced candle-makers err. Here's a very simple way to breathe life into those mishaps—simply wrap them up to create beautiful centerpieces and accents to any room. This is particularly fun at holiday-time, when shops are chock full of wrapping materials: paper, fabric, doilies, foil, etc.

1. Put a piece of wrapping paper on a work surface. Place a candle on its side, up against one edge of the paper. With a pencil, mark a cut line on the paper that represents one-quarter of the way below the top of the candle. Hold the paper against the candle and roll the paper up until the candle is completely wrapped and the paper overlaps by about 1/2 inch. Mark that place on the paper with a cut line.

2. Remove the candle from the paper and use a straightedge to join the cut lines. With scissors or a craft knife, cut the paper along the 2 lines.

3. Wrap up the candle, fastening the paper with a bit of clear tape.

4. Decorate with dried flowers and raffia.

Material for wrapping: paper, foil, corrugated cardboard, paper bags, fabric

Molded candles in a variety of shapes and sizes

Material for decorating: dried flowers, raffia, string, ribbon

resources

BARKER'S ENTERPRISES, INC.
15106 10th Avenue SW
Seattle, WA 98166
(206) 244-1870
Candle-making supplies

BRUSHY MOUNTAIN BEE FARM
610 Bethany Church Road
Moravian Falls, NC 28654
(910) 921-3640 and (800) 233-7929
fax: (910) 921-2681
Beeswax, molds, dyes

CANDLESHTICK
244 Broadway
New York, NY 10024
(212) 787-5444
Waxes, molds, scents, dyes

DEMARLE
2666-B Route 130 North
Cranbury, NJ 08512
(609) 395-0219
Molds

DICK BLICK
PO Box 1267
695 Highway 150 East
Galesburg, IL 61401
(309) 343-6181
Candle-making supplies

FOR THE LOVE OF BEESWAX CANDLES
PO Box 5
Climax, NY 12042
Beeswax products
(518) 731-8303
Beeswax

GLORYBEE
120 North Seneca
Eugene, OR 97402
(541) 689-0913 and (800) 456-7923
Beeswax

MID-CON
1465 North Winchester
Olathe, KS 66061
(800) 547-1392
Molds, scents, dyes

MISSOURI CANDLE &
WAX COMPANY
707 Park Avenue
St Louis, MO 63104
(314) 241-3544 and (800) 894-8531
Beeswax, molds

PEARL PAINT
308 Canal Street
New York, NY 10013
(212) 431-7932
Mail order catalog, general
candle-making supplies

POURETTE
1418 Northwest 53rd Street
Seattle, WA 98107
(800) 888-9425
Candle-making supplies

index

Entries and page numbers in bold refer to individual recipes.
Page numbers in italics refer to photographs.

Acknowledgments

The authors would like to thank
the following for their help
with this book:

Lynn Elfert

Andrea Henley Heyn

Joseph DiPane

Nonie Bauer